吃
chī

（Fourth 弟四 book in the dead man's Kitchen Series）

Eric Moebius Morlin

吃

ISBN:
ISBN-13:

DEDICATION TO: Howard Kunnitz
A grumpy, surly, Damn Yankee Carpet-bagger, and a good friend.
My mom wanted me to invite you to have dinner with them for the holiday.
I can't make it, I'm in China.

321 626 7711
Moebius Guido Machiavelli,
Lump Michael @gmail. Com

—

CONTENTS

	Acknowledgments	vi
1	**You are who you eat**	8
	JiaoZi – Chinese Dumplings	18
2	**Happy Veterans Day**	20
	Peanut Butter Fudge	37
3	**Rage against the Dying of the Light**	38
	Carrot Souffle	42
4	**Beneath the Sands**	44
	Granddad's Pickle Recipe	49
5	**Bella Cum Mortuis**	50
	Mango/Pineapple/ Coconut Bread	56
6	**I've Lived in Worse Nieghborhoods**	57
	Taco Soup	66
7	**It's all Academic**	67
	Spaetzel	80
8	**Wake**	81
9	**Screaming Sobbing Sojourn**	92
	German Potatoe Salad	99
10	**Irish Handcuffs**	100
	Salmon Croquettes	109
11	**Ode to General Tso**	110
	Egg Drop Soup	115

ACKNOWLEDGMENTS

This book wouldn't have been possible without my dad. My dad was an engineer, but he cooked as a hobby. Only to say this could sound dismissive. My dad could literally make a different meal every night for a year, with no sequels. My father ingrained in me a desire for knowledge, and got me reading at an early age. When he started work on his own cookbook, it was to be encyclopedic. He wanted to teach folks about different material components to be used in cooking, like types of sugars and how they are extracted, like a Materia Medica except for cooking.

Even still this book wouldn't have been possible without support from many people, without my mom who gave this angry, ungrateful kid a path to the world, and without the creator of all things, for having breathed life into the whole show to begin with. .

In this book you will see many recipes. I offer all those who put a recipe in my book a free page ad. However, it should also be noted that in the case of many of these recipes they are survivors of another age. For example, Grandpa's Pickle recipe from Jason Goodman, actually comes from his grandfather who is with us no more, but this part of him is preserved in vinegar. The Spaetzel, egg drop soup, and Taco Soup are from my dad. The Mango Bread was inspired by Katherine Kube's experience with banana bread. The Carrot Souffle which is amazing comes from my Aunt Shirley. The Jiaozi recipe from my friend Allen Ju. The Peanut Butter Fudge from my mom.

In the case of some of you it was just moral support, with others financial (buying my books, getting massage, buying my art), spiritual, etc. All too often during the course of this book, I realized that I am a tad bit estranged from myself with grief, and yet… When someone we love dies, they let us see that we don't know where to send the love we had assigned to them, and that pain is all that energy built up inside us and not knowing where to send it, and so we share that love with those around us… While I don't think anyone can "earn love" or be "worthy" of love, I do think that often we are still blessed with it none the less… and I am so grateful for that… I cannot begrudge them, and still honor that…

Nevertheless, loss can drive one Looney Tunes, and searching someone who can raise the dead, when the folks of my own faith seem to have stopped believing and even if they did most would mislabel the source… but none seem to be able to raise the dead. Funny, in a laughter at pain kinda way, funnier still when you laugh and no one else joins in because you crave a resurrection so bad, and… Yeah, you'll notice there are no recipes from Vegans. Several offered, only they never had recipes, even after telling me repeatedly. It was only after I was told by one vegan friend, "I can't deal with the negative energy. I feel like you are trying to manifest the zombie Apocalypse to bring back your ex." I of course then realized the truth was there is an enormous vegan conspiracy wherein they have been feeding on the life force of fellow meat eaters. I realized now the vampiric practices of vegans are somehow responsible for her death, and that if they returned what life force they have stolen off all meat eaters for years, the residual energy would be enough to bring her back…

I would also like to thank: Dorothy Markman, Donna Vigneri, Sherry Ferrel, Charles Stroble, Keith Castillio, Heatherhoney, Paul Cashman, Howard Kunnitz,

吃 chī

Jeremy Frost, David Seaton, Erebus Erudite, Leroy Rob Thompson, Gabby, Edwin Jamison, Ian, Vii Kelly, Daniel James, David Powell, James and Collette Lewis, Billy Blair, Joseph Smihula, Shirley and Ron Carter, John and Tatiana, Tim and Kim, Emily and Abby, Em and Dan, Jen and Robert, Willa and Justus, James and Collette, Bernard Carver, Shane Morton, Cal and Calrissa, Brett, Syd, Rachel Lasiter, Julie Gunter, Ron Wynkoop, Wild Bill, JJ Todd, David, DC, Barrack, Melon, Cat, Mikel Weems, Angie, Kate with and E and Damian, Isis, Logan, Blake Harrison, Suzy and Devin, Temper, Dave, Devon, Cody, Naomi, Tracy Daily, Holly and Adam, Amanda and Jeff, Punk Ray, Becky, Rebeckah, Tami, Chris, Reyna, Becky, Rus, Shannon Holt, Michael Thrush, Andy Lytle, Trey Miller, Kyle, Johnny, Ronne, Lisa, Amanda, Chris, Ian, Nate, Philip Barnett and Jasmine, Chris, Jimbo and Shawn, , TJ Morris and Deborah, Bam Bam, Regina, Johnny and Sarrita, C Word, Eric Brodnax, Brandi Hillman, Dwight Humphries, Lewis Little, Duke Trim, Robert Gunter, Hillary, Ron, Rhea, Joe, Che, Leo Geo, Len, Bailey, Ken Allen, Jesser, Stephanie, Terry, Richard and Lynn Maddox, Kenny Camp, In China: Allan Ju, Charles Yang, Tiger and his Wife Mrs. Tiger, Alfred, Alph, Mrs. Tang, Natalie Wang, Stephen, Tracy, Sophie, Wallace, Lu, and my students who shall remain anonymous, and oh so many others…

1 You are who you Eat

Sept. 27, 2011
Beijing, China

"Learning is not compulsory; it's voluntary... but to survive, We must learn."

—W. Edwards Deming

Rachel arrived at the Beijing airport.

Randal, the school liaison, had met her at the airport with a sign with her name on it.

"Ni Hao," She'd greeted him.

"Hello," He'd replied in English, but with a strong accent, "We need to go to the other airport terminal to pick up another student from South Africa."

She was eager to practice her Chinese, but she could tell he wasn't in the least bit interested. She'd been warned by another teacher Jake

Mcguire, who'd said, "They didn't hire you for your Chinese, and your accent is awful... but you'll find that out soon enough."

Randal took her out to a huge van, and introduced her to another man, Mr. Wang. She tried to speak with him for a moment, before he said, "Bu ting," or "not hear," the equivalent of, "don't understand". She couldn't imagine her accent was any worse than Randal's, but then again... It was a tonal language, and so... the whole language was about accent and inflection.

****

She remembered at that instant something Jake told her," Look you're **Waiguoren**, a foreigner, or... **Waijiao**

Laoshi the foreign teacher. They just want to have you speak English and look good so they can sell the school to the parents of their students.

Learn Chinese, no problem, but don't expect them to understand you, and if they do... Sure they'll be about as excited as if they'd discovered a talking dog, but...

Except expect just as many of them to not understand you, or... if they do, to have it be because they didn't see you when you were talking..."

"Huh? Say what? What do you mean?" She'd asked.

"I'll give you an example. I was in the market, I asked one of the vendors who was working amongst the shelves a question, and he'd been chatting happily away with me, but the moment he turned and saw I was a caucasian... The conversation was over. Suddenly, he couldn't understand a word I said, Bu Ting, bu ting..."

"What do you mean over? You're saying it was like suddenly, he just couldn't understand you because you're white? That's racist as hell," she'd started to say, when Jake interrupted with, "I don't think it's intentional... and it wasn't just him, I honestly just think some Chinese people can't grasp the fact that a white person can speak their language, they shut down..."

"That's the craziest thing I've ever heard," She'd replied.

****

Only here she was, and while her English was a heavily accented tongue that reflected having grown up in Belfast. There was no reason Mr. Wang couldn't understand the few brief words she'd spoken... Unless, and then she found herself doubting everything she knew, which suddenly became... what little she knew.

She'd taken classes for 4 years at Queens College. Of course back then she had been focused on what she felt was her true calling, the Circus School. Only clowning around didn't pay the bills like it used to... and eventually her parents had pushed her to be "realistic" which led to her being a teacher.

Rachel had thought it was the wise and rational decision, but 5000 miles later, and half way around the world to work in China she had started to wonder. I mean, it was perfect timing. She hadn't really listened to the news much before this, but right now... Just as she was arriving China was dealing with some kind of weird respiratory epidemic.

In fact, as Rachel looked around her there were so many people wearing little white hospital face masks. She almost felt like she was in a hospital, or a horror movie. SARS had the city in a panic, and she had to admit, at this moment she felt a twinge paranoid, like she should be wearing a mask as well.

"I will need to file for your work

certificate with the immigration office within 24 hours of your entering the country, but for now we just need to get you settled into your apartment," Randal said in his accented English. It wasn't that he spoke poorly; it was just obvious that his dialect was one derivative of an Asian speaker. It took a lot of work for a person to get rid of such an accent, and for most people it wasn't worth it... that is until they realized how much money it was costing them.

吃　chī

Xiqing District, Tianjin, China

It took almost 3 hours to get from Beijing to Tianjin.

The traffic was strange, the roads were crowded, and often people didn't seem to stay in any particular lane. It didn't feel as chaotic as Roma, or Turkey, but she'd never felt comfortable with the driving in those cities either. When they final got to her apartment building it was late. Randal introduced her to the landlord. The elevator in the building had been out, and her apartment was on the 5th Floor. She was glad however she didn't have an apartment on one of the higher floors.

"The Landlord," Randal said, "says the elevator should be back in service within the next day or so..." She nodded, hoping this would be the case. She was given a sim chip for a cell phone, dealt with gas, electric, and community service fees that were all conveniently taken out of the advance he had for her.

Again she found herself wondering if she'd done the right thing, feeling like she'd just been rolled for her money by the guy who'd helped hire her.

After that however, the two men left, and Rachel settled in for the evening.

The landlord had left her some fruit, some bottled water, a pretty porcelain container full of tea, and a recipe for Chinese dumplings (or Jiao zi). Rachel discovered soon after that all the ingredients were in the fridge waiting for her.

<u>Chinese Jiao zi</u>

(Chinese Dumplings)

500 grams ground beef

1 Scallion

1 ginger root

3 eggs

2 pinches of salt

50 circular dumpling wraps

directions: Mix 1 pinch of salt, and the egg into the ground beef, then cut up the scallion, and ginger into tiny pieces, which should then be mixed in with the egg and beef.

Take a portion of the mixture and place it upon each wrap, then pinch them shut. You may need to add a little egg to the edges of each wrap so they will seal properly.

Now boil water, add a pinch of salt to this water, and put about 10 dumplings at a time into the water, boil for 4-6 minutes.

Next, take the dumplings out with a slotted spoon to dry. You will want to eat them while they are still warm, with some vinegar for dipping.

2 HAPPY VETERAN'S DAY MONTREAL, QUEBEC

Nov 12, 2013

"Anyone who stops learning is old. Whether at twenty or eighty. Anyone who keeps learning stays young. The greatest thing in life is to keep your mind young."

--Henry Ford

Allison woke to being frigid cold, naked, and buried beneath a heavy comforter like you find at some of the nicer chain hotels. This was just the way she liked it. So cold that you had to find your own warmth. She shifted her body around for a moment only to realize that the man she'd been sharing a bed with was no longer there.

Francis... No, Flynn, like Errol Flynn. No wait... it was even better... Rickie Savage, and no, not Rick Savage. Rickie Sav'age with his adorably outrageous French accent.

吃 chī

She just wanted to eat him up…

Yeah, she had.
She thought she could hear him in the bathroom taking a shower. They met the night before on what would have been Veteran's day back home, or what they called Remembrance day in Montreal but by the time they'd gotten back to the room it had been after midnight. Rickie had then jokingly explained to her, "Not to worry, Showers are Time Machines!"
"Wha?" She'd responded.
"Simple my sweet girl, have you ever gotten drunk, and gone to take a shower, only to find yourself climbing out several hours later?!"
Alison laughed, "Sure, only because I…"
"oh lah lah," he'd said interrupting her in a way that was so incredibly cute and sexy, that she didn't kick him in the balls, "time machine," he reiterated.
His logic for this was of course,

questionable, but as often as they traveled back and forth between the shower over the next several hours. She wasn't entirely sure that there might not be some truth to what he'd said, and Allison had been only too happy rock the young man's world, not to mention... her own, ye gods the muscles, on her young Adonis, and while 28 wasn't that old all things considered... It turned out she was lucky she was in such good shape. A younger less experienced woman, might have been overwhelmed, but she'd shown him things, she'd forgotten she knew how to do.

After a moment, Allison figured she'd join Rickie in the shower, only to discover the room empty. The shower steamed the glass of the mirror. Disappointed, Allison showered alone.

Alison had pale skin, almost as white as

the bathroom tiling, an obvious old school goth girl. Rickie on the other hand had told her he was Canadian Special forces. She hoped Rickie wasn't gone for good, and started to momentarily pretend he was with her in the shower, guiding her hand betwixt and between, when she thought she could hear the hotel room door slam…

She quickly finished showering to go out and….

The lights to the hotel room were on and there was blood EVERYWHERE, and revealed in the starkness of the hotel rooms light.

Every light in the room seemed to be on and all the blood, even the bed she'd been dozing in so comfortably moments before looked like it was the scene of some tv forensics show.

Allison pauses a second, "There is no way that's me", she thinks to herself, "My cycle doesn't start up for another…" but then she is interrupted by Rickie who is handing her clothing.

"Get dressed," he tells her. She notices he has a bloody claw hammer in the waist band of his slacks.

Oh, damn I know how to pick 'em," she said to herself, and he'd seemed so nice. There is a fire axe in one of the chairs across the room.

"What the holy happenstance Rickie?" She asks, knowing there can't be any logical explanation, and there he is talking that Montreal patois that always seems more like a elegant way to blaspheme rather than convey actual information, and after a moment when he can tell that she doesn't understand him, rather than just get louder he draws back the curtain to their hotel room, revealing Hell.

She doesn't want to say literally, but what she sees certainly has her asking questions. She almost crosses herself, and she's frikking Jewish. Instead she just gawks for a moment. They are only a few floors up, but the city isn't even the same place she'd seen just before going to sleep. An entire building is gone, like collapsed into the earth pile of smoldering ruins kinda gone…

I mean, sure their sexcapades had been banging, but how could they have not heard that…

She can see bodies sprawled out in the streets. One man is backing his car back over a person he just hit, as if he's afraid they'll get back up.

A store front is on fire and there are pockets of looters and people fighting everywhere… "What the Hell happened?"

She asks again, and Rickie says, "We don't have time for this, get dressed…"

Finally, it comes to a point where Rickie is helping her dress, but she doesn't want to go out, not into the world she's seeing, not into… that.

"I want to stay here," she tells him. Now they can hear yelling on their own floor, a woman's screaming. Rickie says something elegantly blasphemous again, and then, "Please trust me. You don't want me to leave you alone here,"he pauses, "and besides, I am not even sure I could come back and get you…"

"What is this? Is it some kind of terrorist attack," she asks him. And Just then he laughs, and she turns to him, as he says, "I sure to God hope so, I saw…" He starts to say something else then pauses. "I know this will sound crazy, but with so much underground in Montreal people always joked Montreal is secretly a haven for vampires, but…"

Allison says, "Oh, c'mon now. You've gotta know that's mullarkey. You know that right. Vampires don't exist."

"All I know is I… I tried to stop a guy who was attacking a woman with a claw hammer. I've been trained for killing, and… The only thing I got out of that experience… The only thing I know for certain, is we need to leave now!"
"Fine," Allison says, "but I get the fire ax."

It took them several more minutes to prepare. Alison knew she wasn't going to be dragging a big suit case, so that meant dumping most of her clothes, but make up, tampons, all that was considered survival.
Rickie had recovered his service pistol from a duffle bag.
Just as Rickie opened the door to the hallway the woman who had been screaming suddenly fell silent. Rickie raised an open hand in a halt. He stepped out into the hall looking, and then signaled Alison to follow him.

As they started off to the right, Alison looked back down the hall in the other direction. She didn't look for long as she jogged in pursuit of Rickie. She wanted to scream herself but remained silent.

Nevertheless, her brain started to churn out its own narrative. She'd seen three large men fighting over a broken doll in a fluorescent orange sun dress. Alison knew of course, that ts was no doll, nor did she wait to watch what happened next.

The hallway in this direction looked surprisingly undisturbed. The hotel's camera seemed to be patiently recording. A signal to the world that everything was still under control. She wondered if the cameras operators were still there. Watching the world fall apart like it was a movie, or had the gone off to save someone...

The elevators were up ahead, but

Rickie held up his hand again for her to stop. He started to walk forward again but then stopped himself. He looked at Alison, shook his head, and then pointed toward a corridor that led to the snack machines.

Alison could now hear noises from ahead of them, what Rickie had probably heard, and bolted off down the corridor toward the room with the vending machines. She stopped just outside the door which purred with a mechanical hum. She tried opening the big metal door as quietly as she could but it was still loud. As Rickie came up behind her, she expected to see they were being pursued, but… nothing. She was able to keep the door from slamming.

Rickie walked right past her, and the row of vending machines. She wanted to move one of those big bulky soda machines to block the doorway, even as she read the warning not to rock them lest she be crushed.

Now that would be the way to go, crushed to death under a vending machines, as she tried to block a doorway. She knew there was little to no chance she could even move the thing.

Ricky paused before a door marked "Hotel staff Only!" before opening it, to disappear within. Alison didn't know why she didn't follow right after him but as the seconds ticked off. She started to question this decision.

"What if he didn't come back?" she asked herself. Finally, she opens the door only to discover it is a service corridor going off in multiple directions, and… no sight of Rickie. No blood. She listens and she just hears the strangely comforting purr of machinery.

吃 chī

"Oh man," she whispers to herself. She pictures going off down one of the pathways, calling out for Rickie by name, but even as an internal dialogue that goes sideways real fast. She decides to go back and wait… even if only for another ten or fifteen minutes.

There is a heavy duty white plastic table in the room and Alison decides that sitting there will be more comfortable than sitting on cold concrete. Alison decides to try and call someone back home and let them know what is going on. Only to discover her phone isn't getting a signal. Probably because she is in this little concrete vault of a room.

Next she decides that if the world is going to hell in a hand basket she might just want to fill up her bag with as much candy, potato chips, and soda as she can.

It is just over three hours when Rickie walks back through the door from the maintence corridor, and Alison almost accidentally axes him in the face, instead she shoves him across the room, only to pull him back to her by his belt.

"You flaming a'hole! Where were you?," Alison yells, but has to crane her neck to look up at him, and," Why'd you leave me here? Dang it! Never ever do that again!" Rickie can tell he has been properly scolded but now finds himself being kissed on, and in return finds himself feasting on a kisses.

"I'm so sorry. I thought you were behind me, and by the time I realized... yes, there was someone was behind me, but it wasn't you. I started to backtrack, but I ran into a crowd of those things. I've been working to back ever since...

I know we just met, but... Don't think I'd leave you behind though, not ever..."

吃　chī

Properly placated, Alison begins to get her things together leaving a smattering of various snack food wrappers behind. A few last moments before they enter the service passage Rickie does one last review with Alison, of everything he can think of...

"I went left last time. I came back via the tunnel that is straight ahead. If you can't keep up you need to let me know without making too much noise. If you have to, hold my hand. They hear way better than I'd like so... Try not to talk too much," Rickie says.
"uh, why aren't you using," Alison starts to motion as if her hand is a pistol, pointing toward his holstered weapon.
"Oh, I used up all my ammo," Rickie replies with a chuckle, "which leads me to one last thing... something on one of the American television stations. I saw it when I was trapped briefly in a room...

They claim those things are dead like ghouls, and the best way to stop them is to kill the brain."

Alison says, "Now wait, that can't be…"
"You can't deny your own senses baby and you know it," Ricky said, "End of the world **** is going down."
"So, this is going on… everywhere?"
"I don't know," Rickie replies, "but if it's happening here and it's happening in America."
He pauses then, and Alison nods.
Rickie turns then opens the door, claw hammer in one hand, using his foot as a door stop. They then proceed to walk forward quietly, hand in hand.
The maintenance corridors are maze that Rickie seems to navigate effortlessly. Only once do they have a close call entering a room populated with almost a dozen of the dead standing, and turning

to greet them like they'd just interrupted a private conversation.

Rickie managed to get the door closed before they could register being cheated out of a meal, but they weren't going to wait to see if those… creatures? People? Zombies could open doors.

They jog along hallways as lights flicker.
"Can you imagine losing power right now," Alison says, "that would sooo suck…"

Rickie pauses before the next door, he whispers, "stay right here." Alison reaches around to the front of Rickie's crotch and says, "No, you don't want to leave me alone." She then squeezes her hand for emphasis. Rickie's response is, "These are not the droids I am looking for, move along…"
"Oh… I got that. I thought you would have been too young!" and they shuffle through the door together in silence, only

to discover they are in the kitchen of a restaurant. The light is on over a desk toward the back of the room and Rickie walks across the room. "Jackpot," he says softly.

"What? You found a map outta here?! Oh, thank," but that is when Ricky interrupts, "uh, not exactly..."

"What do you mean," Alison says, "You said, Jackpot."

"and I meant it, Hon, just not the way you... thought I meant," Now he sounds sorta sheepish.

"What does it say then," she asks him.

"It's a recipe for peanut butter fudge," Ricky says, "and I love peanut butter fudge."

Alison is silent for a second, then says, "Doesn't everybody... Okay, I'll forgive you, if we survive and you make me fudge, but... ONLY THEN will I forgive you!"

"Deal," Rickie says.

<u>Peanut Butter Fudge</u>

ingredients:
1 cup white sugar
1 cup brown shugar
½ cup evaporated milk
2 tablespoons butter
2 cup small marshmellows
2 teaspoon vanilla
1 1/2 cups peanut butter

Directions:
Take sugar, evaporate milk, butter and stir under on low heat. It sticks easily, and should start to slowly congeal into a soft ball of material floating around in the liquid.

Take off heat and add your marshmellows, vanilla, and peanut butter. Mix this in by hand, and then pour into a pan to cool.

3 RAGE AGAINST THE DYING OF THE LIGHT

National Geospatial Intelligence Agency, Virginia
Nov 11th, 2013

"Contrary to conventional military and game theory, the most effective offense is sometimes a direct attack against your political opponent's greatest strength – not his weaknesses - to place him immediately on the defensive".

- Mark McKinnon

Across the world and in coordination with the **DOD,** the **National Geospatial Intelligence Agency (NGA)** has just taken over **shutter control** of all U.S. commercial and military satellites over the Middle East, India, and Asia. This action might have gone unnoticed if a satellite under the control of **U.S. Africa Command** hadn't been redirected to assist with local communications. The company that operates that small commercial satellite quietly sends out a notice to the Chinese signaling that there has been a "disturbance in the Force" to mix metaphors for a moment.

How? The Chinese own the commercial satellite company being operated by **US Africa command**.

Go figure.

This said, when the **MASINT** from the satellites starts coming in, only one of the operatives on hand is actually able to interpret the data that they are seeing. He is Lt. Barry Whittaker. He walks out of the control room and down the hall to a nearby office.

Inside the office is another Operations center. When he walks in, a few officers sit up to take notice but say nothing. Whittaker sits down at a desk there with a direct line to the office of ▮▮▮▮▮▮▮▮▮▮▮▮▮▮.

"Yes sir, **Advance Geospatial Intelligence** reveals it is worse than we thought, sir," The soldier says into the phone, "**Operation: Seven Vials** is on the table sir."

"I'll inform the President," ▮▮▮ ▮▮▮▮▮ replies, "Have all the **MASINT** forwarded to my office immediately."

"Yes sir," the Lt. responds.

"…and Lieutenant, be reminded that you are to tell no other living soul about what we have discussed," ▮▮▮▮▮▮▮ says.

"Understood sir," Whittaker says, and hangs up.

There is a silence in the room as Whittaker stands and says, "I can tell by the clever banter in the room that you

gentlemen were eavesdropping…
So you know, **Operation: Seven Vials**
is active…

Do you gentlemen need me to tell
you how to proceed?"

One of the men stands, and says, "No,
sir. Our orders are clear…"

"Good. Get to it," Whittaker replies and
walks out of the room without another
word.

What Lt. Whittaker hadn't noticed,
was that today one of his fellow officers
had brought in his mother's carrot
soufflé and they all have tiny plates on
their desks. On the wall in the break
room, he has pasted a copy of the recipe
that looks like it has seen a lot of
attenton over the years.

Carrot Souffle

1 lb baby carrots
1 stick butter
1 cu sugar
3 tbsp flour
1 tsp baking powder
1 ½ tsp vanilla extract

cook carrots until tender in boiling salted water. Drain. Blend carrots and butter in electric blender or mixer until smooth.
Add remaining ingredients and blend well.
butter 1 qt casserole dish, and pour into it. Bake at 350 until set. 45 mins. I cook a bit longer. Serves 6.

Carrot Souffle

1 lb baby Carrots
1 stick Butter (Soften)
3 Eggs, beaten
1 cup Sugar
3 tbsp flour
1 tsp baking powder
1 1/2 tsp. vanilla extract

Cook Carrots until tender in boiling salted water — drain. Blend Carrots + Butter in electric blender or mixer until smooth. Add remaining ingredients + blend well. Butter 1 qt casserole dish + pour into it. Bake 350° until set

45 mins → cook a bit longer Serves 6.

4 BENEATH THE SANDS

███, Afganistan
Nov, 10th, 2013

"That is why one day I said my game will be like the Pythagorean Theorem - hard to figure out. A lot of people really don't know the Pythagorean Theory. They don't them them like me anymore. They don't want to make them like that anymore."

— Shaquille O'Neal

Staff Sergeant Frank Tooler and his platoon had been camped out in and around their Four **Buffalo MRAPs** in the **Green Zone** for a day and a half now, as they were awaiting further orders.

For the Marines that are part of this unit, their vehicle is their lifeline to survival and so, unless compelled by a "higher power", they don't let anyone near them.

Staff Sergeant didn't say he

suspected anyone of being a saboteur, but to his own men he made it perfectly clear he didn't trust anyone who wasn't going out on the road with them; not the locals, not the pope, and not the mercenaries from back home…especially with the mercs, as many of them were known to be connected with smuggling drugs, selling weapons, and in some cases just eliminating the competition…

A guy in khaki shorts, Hawaiian shirt, long white socks, and sandals shows up. His attempt to approach the MRAPS is halted by the Staff Sergeant's men. They make the man wait under the shade of a nearby building.

As Staff Sergeant approaches he is combing back his short black hair. It isn't long by civilian standards, but the men jokingly label it a "winter" cut. The man holds out his hand. They shake hands and, for a moment, the two men stand sweating in the shade as they discuss old hypocrisies in low voices. Finally, Staff Sergeant returns to his vehicles and tells his soldiers that they have escort duty.

One of his men, Jason Hudson, a young fellow from Mississippi, asks, "What about waiting for further orders, Staff Sergeant?".
"Seems that assisting the CIA in smuggling alcohol to our troops is our further orders," the Staff Sergeant responded.

After that the soldiers end up escorting a truck full of booze, and who knows what else to a posh hotel just to the North of ███.

The hotel appears to be more secure than the **green zone**, but "green room" would have suited the mood inside better. The staff sergeant didn't trust the spook from the CIA any more than he trusted anyone else, but didn't want his men to miss out on everything...

Showers, swimming pools, and hookers can go a long way to increase morale. This said, Staff Sergeant only let half his men away from their vehicles at a time. Meanwhile the rest of his crew would go off to shower, get laid, and hang out by the pool. He told his men to keep a careful eye on anyone and everyone , but especially the mercs.

They were involved here just as they'd been in Iraq, but Staff Sergeant wasn't a fan because, as I said before, he'd seen more than a few of them become involved in underground trade, eliminating competing contractors, and even dabbling in arms dealing.

He didn't want his men to be the next casualties.

While the first group of his men take their showers, Staff Sergeant Tooler gets to work on his latest batch of pickles since he'd gone through the trouble to have one of his men collect all the things he'd need earlier in the day.

Granddad's Pickle Recipe:

Ingredients:
6 cups of vinegar
2 cups sugar
6 cups sliced cucumbers
1 cup sliced onion
1 cup cauliflower
1 table spoon mustard seed
1 table spoon turmeric
1 table spoon celery seed

Pickling requires one put the ingredients together in a large pot and boil them until the onions taste good. Usually this is twenty to twenty five minutes.

5 <u>Bella cum mortuis</u>
Somolia
Nov, 11th, 2013

"We do have tendency, now in biology especially to make up stories, to make theoretical biology a kind of game, in fact we have **game theory** in biology which is meant to use the theory of games to make predictions or explain things."

— Richard Lewontin

As **Super Typhoon Yolanda** moved out of the **Philippines**, another storm was moving across the **Arabian Sea** toward **Somolia**. The cyclone labeled **Deep Depression ARB 01** would sweep whole villages away into the nearby **Indian Ocean**.

If you can imagine strands of wind -- unraveling dna strands -- or a storm unweaving houses as if they were woven thread…and the wind works to strip them of all form, all structure….

A young girl named Astur wanders home from visiting her grandparents only to find everything her parents owned had been swept away by the storm. She could still make out the fence that had held in their animals and now the carcasses of those same goats, cattle, and chickens littered the ground.

As yet she saw no human corpse until she saw the others.

Off in the distance, the other villagers were approaching. Astur was thankful, but exhausted, just as many of the villagers appear to be. Most, if not all, moved as if they had grave injuries.

Astur starts to run up to them. She thought she even saw her cousin as she starts to run in closer, only as she approachs, she brushes one of the villagers' arms.

His skin is cold like death.

She knows the skinny, blue black-skinned boy, Aran, and another named Abdi, but they stand gawking, open-mouthed, at her with eyes that seem more focused on the distance shores of the grave. Then one of the boys begins to reach for her and that brief exchange is enough to send the girl running.

Upon noticing her, Aran and the others are slow to react. Soon enough the girl is running for her life. She doesn't know where she might have fled to if there hadn't been the storm, but in the midst of a cyclone she could only flee further inland and away from the water.

...and the dead.

As she runs west, Astur backtracks, making her way back onto the road they had just left. It is the best way back to her grandparent's home further inland. Her grandmother lives across the street from the biggest church she had ever seen. She finally finds her way back to the road leading to the next township.

There is no one on the road in any direction. The girl removes a water bottle from her pack and a piece of her Ayeeyo's Mango bread. Got to keep up your energy.

After a mile or so Astur recognizes a landmark, a huge old tree. She sees her grandmother's home up ahead. It is an old wooden house with a tin roof. The girl almost doesn't want to knock, but... she does.

It is late now, and it takes a moment for her grandfather to light a lantern and come to the door with shotgun in hand.

"Astur, why are you not back at the

village?"
Astur starts to cry, and the elder man
sets the gun to one side and pulls her
through the door and into his arms. He
closes the door quietly after her,
locking it, and for a moment he stands
there with the young grandchild
sobbing in his arms.

Astur tells her grandparents about
the storm, and then about seeing the
dead people walking around. The two
elders don't know what to think.

Luckily, Astur's father had bought
her grandparents a cell phone which
they would rent out during the day
time.

They call a few neighboring villagers
who were part of the local cellular
network. Astur's grandfather tells
them about the storm, but also what
the girl had said about seeing the dead
walk.

Superstition is greeted in one of two ways and, in this instance, it is greeted with laughter and derision. The neighbor says he will confirm if any of what the young girl said is truth. When he calls back a short while later, he never gets back on the phone line, rather the call ends with his screaming, and then not exactly silence, as there are other strange noises in the distance; ones that sound horrible and strangely familiar.

Afterwards her family cuts her a slice of Ayeeyo's Mango bread and they put the girl to bed. This relic is her grandmother's recipe:

MANGO / PINEAPPLE / COCONUT BREAD

2 STICK OF BUTTER & 2 CUPS SUGAR
BLEND / MIX WELL
ADD MANGO - APPROX 1½ cups & 1
small CAN dRAINED PINEAPPLE
MIX WELL
ADD 4 EGGS MIX WELL
ADD 1 CUP OF FLAKE COCONUT &
MIX WELL.

IN SEP. CONTAINER MIX
2 3/4 cup of FLOUR
2 TSP OF BAKING SODA
1 TSP SALT.

SIFT INTO MANGO MIXTURE
MIX WELL.
PUT IN 2 GREASED LOAF PANS

BAKE 350° FOR 1 HR.

6 I've lived in Worse Neighborhoods
Berkley, CA
Nov 10, 2013

"Socialism violates at least three of the Ten Commandments. It turns government into God, it legalizes theivery, and it elevates covetousness. Discussions of income inequality, after all, aren't about prosperity but about petty spite. Why should you care how much money I make, so long as you are happy?"
--Ben Shapiro

It was a riot. This isn't to say Paul wasn't having a good time. He was, but it was also... literally a riot. Don't be surprised... Berkley is alot like those places in Europe full of "oppressed" people who just so happen to be living in a place that affords them a better standard of living than most of the rest of the world.

Of course, Paul revels in the utter hypocrisy a state that "cares so much" about the environment but then dumps millions of gallons of super salinated salt water into the ocean poisoning the coast line, and then there's compasssionate California's infrastructure supposedly designed to look after the poor and the disenfranchised. They just can't afford to live there.

Paul certainly wouldn't be able to if he wasn't couch surfing at a friend's house in San Francsco, and he knows that isn't going to last.

He landed a job at a coffee shop in the upper Haight, but he can't afford to rent anything for anything even half way reasonable, unless he would be willing to pretend like he's trans, because those "welcoming and loving" communal living folks, only have "open welcoming arms", for folks who are black, gay, or trans.

"The oppressive whites", he's been told, " are wealthy, established, and working for a software company", and there was plenty to be said for locals being insular and looking out for their own, but everyone seemed to pretend there aren't just as many poor struggling whites.

Whatever the case, he was here rioting with everyone else, in a moment of shared pseudo-solidarity protesting the destruction of a local park, for Paul it was just an excuse to get out some of his exististential angst by breaking stuff and stealing stuff.

Where else are you going to be able to get away with the sheer mayhem.

Paul watched the mob in front of him move down the street, people throwing bottles and rocks. The police hung back on side streets making sure the destruction was contained to the main strip.

While others marched down the street throwing bottles, and rocks. Paul picked up a newspaper despener and smashed a car windshield. It felt good to be alive.

It is ironic that this is the exact moment he looked over to see a huge biker guy stabbing someone in the face. The biker guy was already bloody and it looks like the other guy might have bitten him, but the raw brutality of watching him. Paul recognized the guys colors, and started to curse out loud. He knew out of all the times in his life where he could keep his mouth shut, now it was more nessecary than ever. He took off running in the opposite direction of the rioters, toward the nearest Bart station, and didn't look back. He had just seen someone murdered and there was no way he couldn't recognize the name of the motorcycle club on the back of the guys vest. He just had to go back to Noreen's place, and crash out, pretend like tonight never happened.

Only as he got closer and closer to the BART he kept seeing people fighting everywhere, and weirder still, alot more people biting people. The station was empty. Paul knew the riots might put people off from riding the BART, but he'd never seen it so... barren. He ran straight to the platform for Warm Springs/Feemont.

The trains run every 20 minutes, so Paul wasn't waiting long, but in that time... No one else arrived to catch a train. When the train pulled into the station he saw three guys he knew, and their girlfriends. The way they were all dressed, Paul knew they were heading for the riots. It was like they were all going out for a date. It made him question his own sanity for a moment, because he knows it will mean missing the train.

He run over, "Hey guys, Hold up." Alex Freeman, a black skater kid from Oakland greets him, "Paul! Homes! Good to see you I was wondering if you were coming out tonight!"

"Good to see you too man," Paul says, now wondering if he is being too paranoid as he says, "You guys don't want to go out there tonight..."

He pauses and silence fills the space between them like the room was suddenly flooded with it...

An asian kid whose "English" name he now remembers to be Jason intones sarcastically, "What's a matter, the cops use a itty bit of the big bad tear gas? C'mon man, quit being a..." and then pauses to look at his girlfriend and continues, "Don't be a wuss man..."

"Grow some what?" His girlfriend intrupts.

"I saw a guy get stabbed, and there are a bunch of crazy assholes out biting people. Do what you want, I'm just trying to give you the heads up."

Alex says, "Is it really that bad?"

Jason and a couple others actually groan out loud. This time it's a Latino kid named Saul says, "Oh, Alex man?! Are your really gonna chicken out just because your caucasian homie here says, you should be frightened... Jason is right, you need to grow some Cahones." He then looks at Paul, and says, "No offense bro."

Paul laughs, partially because he totally

knows, Saul is trying to offend him. Second, he knows Saul doesn't speak Spanish. He is Latino by heritage, but his family has already been assimilated.

"No, by all means, find out for yourself," Paul says. Alex puts his hand up to his friends in a gesture of hold on a second, and whispers to him, "I trust your judgment, but I can't look weak in front of my girl... I'll call you later." Paul says, "I understand, "knowing he'd probably do the same thing if he hadn't been out there tonight.

The next train arrives on time, and he climbs aboard awaiting. He walks into the train to sit when suddenly he hears someone yelling from across the BART terminal. He runs toward the doors of the train just in time to see them close shut. He tries to wedge the doors open, as he looks out to see Alex and the others running toward the train, but there is nothing he can do... except perhaps stop the train.

He now realizes that one of the girl's looks injured, like perhaps she'd been bitten, and Jason is nowhere in sight. This is the last thing he sees of them, as the trains speeds away, and the disappear from sight behind him.

It is then that he notices there is a note card of some kind on the seat beside him. He picks it up, only to discover it is a recipe.

TACO SOUP

2 15 OZ CANS HOMINEY
1 1.25 OZ. PACKAGE TACO SEAS
2 15 OZ. CANS GREAT NORTHERN BEANS
1 28 OZ CAN CRUSHED TOMATOES
1 11 OZ. CAN NIBBLETS SWEET CORN
1 15 OZ CAN RANCH STYLE BLACK BEANS
1 14 OZ. CAN ITALIAN ROTEL TOMATOES
1 1.25 PACKAGE TACO SEASONING
1 1OZ ENVELOPE HIDDEN VALLEY RANCH
   SALAD DRESSING MIX
2 LARGE ONIONS CHOPPED
3 POUNDS GROUND BEEF

BROWN GROUND BEEF, DRAIN THE FAT IN A
LARGE POT ADD ALL THE INGREDIENTS
INCLUDING THE LIQUID IN THE CANS, ADD
TWO CUPS OF WATER AND SIMMER FOR A
HOUR AND A HALF.

7 IT'S ALL ACADEMIC

Ranch, Montana

Nov. 12, 2013

"The ultimate value of life depends upon awareness and the power of contemplation rather than upon mere   survival."

--Aristotle

Marlowe had been on lock down for almost 24 hours. Okay, that isn't entirely true. He was gaming. The folks at home office knew yesterday was his day, and that meant he wasn't available even if the world ended.

Ironically, Marlowe was pretty sure that his employers didn't think he actually meant it when he told them he would be unavailable even if the world ended, and now 24 hours later....

It was getting to be around that time, when duty calls. For gaming he was running on an older system, a ███████████ partially because he could keep it 100% offline without all the game updates, which might require hours of game time between updates.

He hated updates. It was the reason he hadn't even considered the newer game systems and it wasn't because he didn't have bandwidth out to the ranch. It is, however, what he told folks in town…

It wasn't like he didn't know the world had gone to Hell in a proverbial handbasket but, so far, he couldn't see it on his end and he, true to his word, didn't let it interfere with his gaming. Which is the other reason his game system isn't plugged into the net, and in fact it is probably the ONLY thing in the ranch house that isn't on grid. This was solely because he hated being pressured into working on game days…

Of course, on days like today everyone wants his attention. Marlowe is a firm believer in helping cultivate in others a deep appreciation for services rendered, only sometimes he feels he's too good at his job. Normally they had someone who should have covered for him.

As network administrator running services for some very "special people with special needs", whose needs sometimes include accessing **Mass spectrographic intelligence (Massint), Geospatial intelligence (Geoint)** from satellites, and **UAVs**, drone strikes, and what have you signaling to military or paramilitary forces the location of a target…

Marlowe ended his 24-hour gaming session and started to look over yesterday morning's network traffic.

It seems things had really started to go sideways once he went back to gaming based on **Sigint** among other things. Marlowe knew just how bad it was.

He was pretty sure he wasn't going to be getting a paycheck, not because he wasn't going to have a job, but rather there might well be no one left living for whom to work.

Field offices across the globe reported the same crazy ass things from the **Phillipines** to **Sierra Leone**, **Atlanta** to **London**: dead people, or seemingly dead people, attacking and eating the living

Other encrypted transmissions that he could only glean small bits of information from suggested this was **Operation: Brushfire** all over again;

except on a global scale.

Ironically, Marlowe hadn't seen this many operations on the board since the day before 9/11. Not only that, this time they are also seeing a shortage of support staff. Literally no one at the "home office" is picking up and he is anything except leadership material.

I mean, it had to be a prank right? Either that or it is the first 48 hours of the zombie apocalypse and he'd had fast food delivered to his house a half dozen times without the driver mentioning anything…which isn't to say it wasn't possible.

One would think one of the delivery drivers would have mentioned something or noticed something was going on. Was it possible, the area just rural enough, that they had been able to avoid the largest brunt of the disease? Sure,

but…
The main gate to the ranch house
was built to the same specifications as
the rest of the property so he didn't
actually have to meet the driver. He
could have just put the money in a
turn style and taken the pizza, but
instead he went out to the caged
entrance so he could talk to the guy,
listen for observations, gage
reactions….
Nada.
Marlowe wonders for a moment if
it is possible to spoof that much
internet traffic at once in order to
organize a massive zombie
apocalypse hoax.
He still isn't sure.
Whatever happened, ██████
Ranch is built like a fortress from the
main building to the accessory and
out buildings to the hangars further
in, and everything was built to

withstand what was coming.
Everything was blast hardened to take
a Predator strike, or worse..

Marlowe starts answering queries
for other offices as well as accessing
███████ intranets for various
facilities to pull up the security
camera feeds. In dozens of offices it's
business as usual in Birmingham,
Alabama and same for the one in the
U.K. In fact, in dozens of offices
across the globe nothing is amiss.
Only Marlowe has been looking at
all their field offices, warehouses,
safehouses, private hangars, etc... It
isn't typical to see so many of them
empty. His employers make as much
off of selling intel as they do with
"protection services" and that requires
someone to be on call.
Other offices look like they are still
decorated for Halloween, all dead

bodies and viscera. The rooms look like they've been painted in what you'd hope is corn syrup and red food coloring.

Seeing the video feeds prior to his gaming sabbatical reveals a different story. Those folks are dead. He watches to see people he has worked with, albeit usually not in person, getting torn apart before his eyes. Shelly, a station manager in Port-au-Prince, looks like someone made her into pulled pork. He sees the Station Chief at one of the facilities posed on his desk with a femur cradled in his arms like a baby.

How it is that other facilities haven't noticed all this going on makes Marlowe review data feeds from around these townships just to see if they're slacking or if somehow the contagion had skipped them entirely.

Marlowe codes in the signals for a total lockdown of all facilities, but he knows once people realize what has happened they won't want to abandon their families and friends to what is waiting for them.

When that is done, Marlowe starts to review the data to figure out where the folks that are "out of the office" went. There are over a dozen teams of operatives that went on missions never to return.

In other instances it is merely an issue of the staff having been trapped in another part of their own facility when it went on lockdown. Normally, the home office should have freed most of them hours ago.

Of course, with the home office MIA the chain of command would have normally been diverted to him. He finds himself mouthing the words "Not on game day" with far less vehemence than he might normally feel when it probably would have been more appropriate had he said "Not on my watch". He knows that if he hadn't been dicking around, then many of those now dead might have survived.

D'oh.

Luckily for him, it looks like the folks who might have faulted his actions seem to be offline. He can't even access the camera at central, but he knows eventually he'll need to find a way through.

A few facilities have folks trapped in access corridors, laboratories, or apartments. Several of the individuals, being competent agents, have managed to break into other parts of their building, sometimes to their detriment as they stumble into the reason the building had been on lockdown in the first place. In many cases it did not end well. Now at least Marlowe feels like he might be able to reroute some of these busy little beavers.

When Marlowe finally is able to access central, he can get to additional security feeds and start opening doors to allow agents into other parts of their facility, being sure to direct them away from places that need to remain quarantined.

A stationwide lockdown wasn't a bad idea in theory, but without someone to coordinate it…

Marlowe wishes the home office was responding. He would have much preferred that the folks back at the office should be handling all this, but is still unable to get them on the com.

A tactical team is trapped in an elevator in San Paolo. The station chief there is an unusually large man and is compromised. From reviewing the camera feed, it looks like he had a heart attack.

The tac team in the elevator probably could have gotten out on their own, but by taking control he'll also have some operatives back in play. That is, if this is something from which folks can actually recover. Marlowe was the ephemeral ghost in the machine but he had to be careful about that, too, not letting others know where he is working from, rerouting IP addresses, using a VPNs. He implements his SWARM to create false traffic so other operatives see there are other people communicating creating the illusion of everything being as it should. His perspective is he is creating in them a psychological sense of stability by helping them believe someone is still

in charge; even if it is a dirty rotten,
no good… lie.
He also triggers the DHARMA
protocols which will help delete his
presence from the internet, unless
they really know where to dig.

It is then, that he notices, an email
from a buddy of his from Krautville.
Oh, don't tell him that… He doesn't
like Marlowe's humor, but it does
seem he was kind enough to send him
something he'd asked for… A recipe
he remembers from his childhood.

13

SPAETZEL
  BY BOB MARKMAN
  8-29-93

1 C. FLOUR (REGULAR)
1 EGG
1/2 TSP SALT
3/4 C. MILK (DEPENDS ON THE FLOUR)
1/2 STICK BUTTER(REAL)
SEASONED ITALIAN BREAD CRUMBS

HAVE POT OF WATER AT <u>GENTLE BOIL.</u> CUT
SPAETZEL WITH A KNIFE INTO WATER APPROX
1" THICK. WHEN FLOATS TO THE TOP IT
SHOULD BE READY. SPOON OFF INTO BIG
BOWL, SPRINKLE WITH SEASONED ITALIAN
BREAD CRUMBS. CONTINUE TILL ALL OUT OF
BATTER. BROWN BUTTER & POUR OVER THE
SPAETZEL FOR A TRULY DELECTABLE FEAST
(PER EMILY AND ALL OF US.)

吃　chī

8 **WAKE**

Atlanta, Georgia
Nov, 13th, 2013
"A man who wastes one hour has not discovered the value of life."
---Charles Darwin

Mack comes into the house that morning in his favorite fluffy orange bathrobe and holding the the sawzall. There are a dozen people camped out back and a dozen more are all sleeping around the living room. Some sleep on couches, some on the floor; but it is obvious no one wanted to go home.

Mack sees Shelby standing in the hall that leads back to their -- or his -- room. Shelby is still dressed in the same clothes she wore the night before.

"I tried not to wake you up," Mack starts to say.

"What with your yelling about there being no hot water?" Shelby says, then playfully, "I didn't hear any of that."

Mack suddenly finds Shelby has moved into his arms. He pulls her in tight thinking, "Finally", as if this moment completed some higher purpose. He doesn't ever want to let her go. Mack knows he is supposed to go into work, but his truck was being driven by his boss so it isn't like he was going to get fired.

"The water ain't gonna be hot for another 35 or 40 minutes," Mack says.

"I guess you'll have to do something to keep me occupied until then," Shelby says.

"I…uh….," Mack starts to say, and Shelby turns to point

at him, then makes a shh sign with her fingers, then points with her head toward the bedroom. Mack can't help but follow.

They start kissing before they get through the doorway. Mack helps Shelby out of her shirt and removes her bra with the quick flick of his fingers. Shelby is sucking and biting on his nipples, her tongue flicking in and out of her mouth. She reaches down to wrap her fingers around his cock only to discover it already standing resolute.

At that moment Mack reaches down to sweep her off

her feet and into his arms, and he carries her into the bedroom.

Once in the bed, Mack slides Shelby's blue jeans off of her. She is wearing some teeny tiny underwear and he slingshots them across the room. Her legs are so pale they are almost white, and her pubis is shaven clean.

As he kneels between her legs, Mack begins to spell out words with his tongue against her clit. It is a free style of words that he will never dare to whisper to her. He kisses the lips of her vulva as her fingers push into herself.

All the while he is exhaling

sonnets and she is gasping with pleasure, gasping for life.

He licks and sucks at her pussy until finally she can take no more. Mack has no hair to grab, so she latches onto an ear, and pulls him to her.

"Now," she says.

Mack starts to push into her, but pauses.

"What?" he asks, just barely inside her, but slowly starting to pull back out. Shelby screams out, "You need to fuck me! NOW!" She grabs his ass cheeks in both hands and a finger nail cuts into his ass cheek, drawing blood as she pulls him toward her.

Mack slides into Shelby, feels the muscles of her vagina squeezing against him as he pushes in. He pushes in until Shelby cries out, and then he starts to pull back, only to push in deeper.

They begin grinding into each other. Mack has Shelby's legs up by her head as he tries to push into her deeper. She howls out to him, her words unintelligible, almost alien, as if she were speaking in tongues. He can feel as she starts to soak through the bed.

He continues to push into her, finding that silent rhythm shared only between them. She has started to kiss on his hand as he pushes into her and to suck on his finger tips. The roughness of his hands contrast with her smooth softness, and he finds himself on a bridge to an earlier time they shared together.

Lying out in the square back when they still had a park, his eyes closed, but still feeling the warmth of the sun behind closed eyes, his head in her lap, and her brushing her fingers through his hair. He'd yearned for her to hold him again, to give him children.

In such a world like this he knew such children would be powerful. He knew they'd be strong…

"Oh, my," he starts to say, suddenly feeling like all the world was brought into focus, where their bodies meet, and…

"yes, that's it," she whispers

"SO close," he tells her, and that's when he feels a hand slide back to wrap around him like she was ready to milk his essence into her…

"Wife," he says, then to himself, *Oh, Lord, what have I done?.* I mean, not that the good Lord might not have wanted him to make her an honest woman, but…that just isn't what you say to a girl the first time you ever have sex with her. People go all high drama. At that exact moment his orgasm rushes into her. …but to speak such intimacies with a woman you barely know, excepting in the Biblical sense, is generally folly.

吃 chī

"Husband," she says, and both are pulled out into the depths of the rumblings of orgasm.

9 <u>Screaming Sobbing Sojourn</u>

West Palm Beach, Fl
Nov 11, 2013

"Only those who dare to fail greatly can ever achieve greatly.".
– Robert F. Kennedy.

Brock Warren sat with his old lady, Laura, in the front lobby of the abortion clinic. Brock was a big guy and next to him Laura, who stands 5'11", looks small next to him. Laura has long brown hair and green eyes.

In order to get into the clinic they had to walk through a mob of really miserable human beings.

Brock could empathize that if he perceived human life as having value then a child would mean genetic diversity which a species needs in order to survive, but....

He isn't quite sure he hasn't given up on the human race, so.... So, what is one more life? So he thinks all this, almost ironically because, even if he can understand the reason why they think what they do, he finds their approach reprehensible. Only Brock knows this reaction is in part because he is so detached from his own emotions.

So, when Brock and Laura had arrived at the clinic no one stood in their way. Brock moved through the crowd outside the clinic as if they weren't even there, as if Brock thought, "They agreed with Laura", and thought, 'Thank God that monster isn't going to be allowed to breed.'" Yet all the while the crowd was full of froth at the mouth with vitriol. As it was, the crowd seemed to turn its gaze from Brock and Laura.

When they arrive at the clinic, it is much the same. Brock identifies himself and says they have an appointment and they are let in immediately. Not even the usual you-need-to-fill-this-form-out business in the lobby.

When another woman who was waiting starts to protest, Brock locks eyes with the woman and she stops dead in her tracks like an animal sensing it has encountered a predator and fight-or-flight has delivered them as a delicately wrapped meal before the wolf.

Brock and Laura have been together for over a decade now. He knows she didn't want kids. She admitted she was basically selfish. She doesn't want to spend the time, energy, or love on anyone.

When she told him she was pregnant but wanted an abortion, she knew Brock believed that this was how you traveled eternity, and was expecting a fight.

Only Brock had said, "No, I get it, hon. It's reasonable that you don't want to have a child with someone you don't love." She had kinda hemmed and hawed after that, and said, "I just hate children. I just see all these smarmy kids' inexperience. I hate their stubborn and ready-to-make-mistakes-'cause-they-can't-believe-anyone-else-might-know-much-of-anything-attitude. Kids that don't know their history or even why you'd need to know it…"
"If it's like that," he'd said, "we don't have to raise our kids to be uneducated." Brock noticed she didn't deny she didn't love him just as she herself noticed the same.
"At least you didn't say, yeah, you didn't love those other kids, because they weren't yours, but when it's your kid…it's different," she says.
"Would you consider another

option?" Brock asked.

"Ah, here we go," Laura says, "Did you have to wait until we got to the clinic to do this?"

"You want to cut that thing out of your guts and eat it, I'm gonna support your decision," Brock says, "Heck, I might even have a slice…"

Laura interrupts, "Brock!"

"I just…. What if there was another option that wasn't adoption or abortion? What if you didn't have to have the kid but the world still had all the knowledge of that genome, like we still protected the genetic diversity of the species?" Brock asks.

"…Uh, try again," Laura says, "What exactly are you asking?"

"Would you be willing to let the doctor freeze your embryo instead of killing it?"

"Wait. What?!" she begins to ask.

"There are couples who can't have

kids on their own. It would be worth fifty grand if you sold the embryo," Brock says.

"What? Wait. I thought you were against this kind of thing," she says.

"I ain't ever against making money," he tells her.

What makes it all so strange is that Brock didn't remember anything after that. Then there's the fact that he should find himself walking down Clematis Street this many hours later. A building is burning nearby and there is a loud keening whistling like a tea kettle going off in his head. He looks to see a woman standing by the side of the road screaming. The woman's garments are torn and bloody just like his own. Warren realizes just then that his arms, his clothing; they all look like they'd been tye dyed in blood…and where is

Laura?

He is a couple blocks down the street from a local bar called Respectables. He knows exactly where he is. Now just to figure out how to get back.

"I'd never have hurt Laura", he whispers. Only as he is trying to reassure himself; his clothes are drenched with blood. He has to go back to the clinic or turn himself into the police.

At the exact moment, Brock looks down to see something is stuck to the bottom of his shoe. It is a recipe for German Potato Salad.

German Potato Salad
ingredients:
5 lbs potatoes
2 or 4 large onions
1 cup vinegar
1 cup water water
1/2 cup corn oil
½ cup olive oil
Directions:
Boil potatoes in skin in salt water. Steam dry, peel, cut up into 1/4 thickness. Put everything is a good, sealable seasonings container. This should have your water, vinegar, and oil already in it. Add potatoes to mixing container.   Pepper to taste.

10 **Irish Handcuffs**
Nov. 21, 2013
Glasgow, Scotland

"In Madness I thought I was the most important man in the world."
                              --- John Forbes Nash.

Jordie has been running on no sleep for 3 days now. He has been directing everyone from a post atop the roof of their high flat atop Glenavon Rd. Here Hammish had set up a broadcasting station in the outbuilding, and so Jordie had been sitting on the roof with a big plush leather chair from one of their secretly posh, and nowhere to be found neighbor.

Gregor had set up a keg of Guinness, and cigarettes were given out every morning. One pack per person. Between the lads from his old football team and recruiting amongst survivors in the neighborhood, there were thirty of them. This isn't to say there were thirty people in the building, but thirty people composed the core group of people Jordie knew well enough to depend on. There were people he could entrust to other tasks, but the point being was that this was a three-carton-a-day habit for their group alone.

In the rest of the building and surrounding buildings there were 287 people. Jordie had been having Donnan, Gregor and Finley go door-to-door and floor-to-floor, first checking for survivors, and second to find out how many folks they would need to feed and take care of.

Donnan and Gregor were wearing the armor they'd taken from Kelvingrove. Finley had swords, but wore his normal attire of jogger bottoms and a hoodie.

There were approximately 121 flats per building and three buildings. Out of 363 flats 130 of them were empty of people. It wasn't that no one had rented them, but rather they were the tenants who never returned. No one knew if the occupants had gotten trapped somewhere, had abandoned the city, or had just up and heeded the call to rapture...or worse.

Jordie had grown up with that view from the rooftop. He always loved being able to look over the Western Necropolis, and then go to the other side and be able to see cars burning in Maryhill.

Now looking over the Necropolis makes him feel like he has been seeing the true heart of the whole city all along.

The dead number in the tens of

thousands in some parts of the city. In those places they remind him more of insects than humans in some places They are like army ants trying to devour everything in their path.

Hammish and Finley come up the stairs. Finley pours himself some Irish handcuffs.

He walks over to where Jordie stands. There are fires raging all over the city.

"We got the roads clear on the street," Finley says.

"Yeah, but have you seen what's going on by Blackhill Rd?" Jordie replies.

"We'll get there," Finley replies.

Jordie laughs suddenly, and says, "Forgive me brother, I'm knackered, and...I gotta say I'm probably a wee bit mad wae it." He gestures toward a half dozen empty pint glasses.

"Well, fak ye ole geezer, bolt ya

rocket then," Hammish interjects, but he does this in a playful manner, clapping Jordie on the shoulder. Then, "Go to bed. We have it covered. We won't launch any crazy offensives, and we won't let Frazier start another Moltov war ."

Jordie half smiles, and nods, "Good night."

"God bless, and No bar fights," Hammish says, reminding them of older, better times.

"God bless," Jordie mumbles, "and no bar fights."

He drags himself off to bed.

As Jordie goes down one floor to his flat he thinks of what they'd accomplished. In their scheme they had established stability.

Jordie had tried to conceal their success from the rest of the city; he had his people blacking out windows. Only they'd already had scavengers attempt to hit them several times. One of the older tenants, a veteran, revealed he had a stockpile of World War II weapons.

They had replaced and reinforced doors; they had cleared nearby streets and blocked them off with almost a dozen lorries. Jordie was exhausted just thinking about it. All the work they had done, and were yet to do …

The next thing on the list is for Hamish and Frasier, who were going to construct protective barriers on each floor so that if one of the pensioners did have a heart attack or something, they wouldn't have free reign in the building.

Quite a few of the geezers who'd barricaded themselves away had survived and, as they recovered, they joined in the "war effort" as it were, by making food stuffs for "the boys", as they now called them.

"Aw for fucks sake," Jordie says to himself aloud, remembering he'd told one of the widows he'd come get the salmon croquettes she'd made.

"Gaun yerself," Jordie says, forcing himself to turn around and back toward Mrs. Backrie's apartment. She is three floors down, and it is a brisk jog. Jordie thinks they are all going to need to institute some kind of fitness program or something, too.

Jordie opens the door to the stairwell and into Mrs. Backrie's open arms. Sweet Mrs. Backrie manages to bite him right on the tit before he can do anything about it.

"Pish," Jordie says to the old woman in his arms. It is like they are dancing as he smashes her head against a nearby wall.

Jordie then proceeds to walk down to Mrs. Backrie's apartment. Her door is open and it doesn't appear that she encountered anyone else on the way. Small favors. Jordie goes inside the old woman's apartment and locks the door. He then proceeds to write a note to the lads.

Dear Gentlemen and you to Savages (trying to keep things lighthearted here...):

It seems I was correct to want transparent barriers around stairways, and dividing halls. So, if one turns as their going out for the night, then they'll get stuck, hopefully. No regrets. We hadn't scheduled the work until tomorrow, so no blaming yourselves. I have locked myself in Mrs. Backrie's apartment. As I hope you all value my opinion, I hearby nominate Hammish to take my place running things with Finley as second. Also, I ate all the salmon croquettes. You guys really missed out, but here's the old bird's recipe. God bless and no bar fights,

Jordie

He then slid the note out into the hallway and proceeded to eat everything even vaguely satisfying in the woman's house. The salmon croquettes were amazing.

Salmon Croquettes
ingredients:
1 large can salmon (drained)
onion flakes, salt & pepper to taste.
2 beaten eggs
½ cup buttermilk
½ cup flour
¼ tablespoon soda
directions:
Mix together the drained salmon with the seasoning, eggs, milk, and flour mixed with soda. Fry to a golden brown, turning once. Serves 6 to 8.

11 Ode to General Tso

November 7, 2011
Tianjin, China

"Libraries, public parks, art, police, fire brigades, places of worship, roads, bathhouses, public cisterns... All these things could be considered as, for the public good, or even labeled benevolent self interest, and they existed long before socialism, but that is what socialists do... They steal credit for other people's ideas, and the products for other people's labor, and if you know someone who claims to be one they're either a desperate, a mooch, or a wanna be a mooch, or their profiting off the suckers who bought into it, but... don't expect them to cut you a check..."

--William Andrew Davis

Rachel waited for the bus to school. It was cold out, or as the locals would say, "hen leng..." (sounds like: hen lung) only this wasn't why she felt bad. On Thursday night she had gone to the local market on Wan Xue Lu, and while there she'd bought some Kimchi, and some tuna... Canned, nothing fancy or risky. She'd eaten dinner late, gone caught the bus for school, eaten breakfast, and gone through her day… Only when she'd gotten home she started to feel sick, and it felt like food poisoning.

Now, Friday about half the student body was also sick with some kind of cough, that came with fever, and chills… Which with the whole SARS thing had her paranoia in overdrive, but then to be hit by some kind of stomach virus… I mean, it seemed too much time to have been food poisoning, and she'd never heard from food poisoning from Kimchi, but…

Anyway, she come home, felt like she might be sick, run to the toilet and found herself in a very unlady like position. Let's just say, she ended up very dehydrated very quickly. She felt like she was going to die, which meant a lot of praying… which she hadn't done in quite some time.

Now, back to school, business as

usual. The kids were the same way, they could be coughing, have fever, yellow phlegm, and they were still coming to school like it was expected of them. Which... considering how hardwork seemed to be engrained in asian culture. It probably was... but it also mean that if one person was sick, whatever was causing it burned through the population, and if it was this SARS thing...

Today she wore a face mask, she'd bought it after reading how bad the pollution here in Tianjin really was... She'd thought it was just fog, but then realized... not the case.

All this sounds so bleak, but on the positive side she had met several awesome people since she'd arrived. One was a couple that ran a local restaurant. A guy who jokingly had introduced himself to her as Dragon, but whose real name was Jun Fei something or another. It made her think of that story about the martial artist guy Wong Fei Hong, maybe… anyways. Doesn't matter. She calls him Dragon, and his wife who was never introduced to her officially… She thinks of as Mrs. Dragon. Both of them are super sweet, and try to talk to her using the translator on her phone. She figures that her Chinese really must suck, because even when she says something in a way that she is sure is correct, they ask her all sorts of questions that tell her they didn't hear it… Either that, or everyone here is just really good at F'ing with people.

The next person she met was Grace. Grace was a engineer at a local computer company and when she'd found out that Grace was home and sick as hell she'd come over with egg drop soup. Having good friends certainly made it easier to navigate hard times.

The school bus is practically empty, and she knows the classrooms are going to be just as bad. Still there are a couple kids on the bus hacking away, and looking like they feel miserable.

Rachel decides not to eat breakfast and starts to walk up the stair that lead to her classroom. She isn't sure why, but Chinese culture sees schools beings as being these huge constructs... The taller the better, and the older the kids got, the higher they had to climb. There was a strange romanticism there, if you weren't the one having to climb five flights of stairs to get to work every day.

It was around the third floor that she reached into her pocket, and discovered a letter. When she opened it and started to read, she found

herself chuckling aloud, and said,
"Grace." This is what she found.

13
EGG SOUP
  BOB MARKMAN 10-24-77

2 BEEF BOULLION CUBES & 1 CHICKEN
2 C. WATER
1 T. FLOUR
1 EGG

ADD BOULLION CUBES INTO 1-1/2 C WATER,
BRING TO A BOIL .
MIX FLOUR WITH 1/2 C. WATER.
WHEN BOILING ADD FLOUR MIXTURE AND
BEATEN EGG.

ABOUT THE AUTHOR

Eric Moebius Morlin is a Florida Native. He ran away from home at 16 to live on the streets in Atlanta, Georgia for the next 14 years. During the decade that followed Moebius ended up working for Dragon Con, and became entrenched in the Atlanta as a street performer in the Little Five Points community.

Little Five Points was unlike anything Moebius had experienced before the people in the neighborhood had a community that seemed to be unbound by traditional social conventions... This isn't to say it was all good, or paradise by any stretch of the imagination. There were a lot of bad, even fuck up things that transpired during those years... Suicides, overdoses, murders, killings... Counter culture offers a buffet of bad choices, and Moebius made as many bad choices as he did good ones.

In 1998, Moebius was awarded the Creative Loafing's Most Interesting Street Personality: Critic's Choice. Not that anyone at the magazine actually spoke to him. He is still waiting for them to review one of his books. Back then he made his living by reciting, "Poetry for your Spare Change, or your watch".

In 2001 Moebius's Dad got Sqamous Cell Cancer and he moved back home to help take care of him. Since that time he has gone on to earn an Associates Degree at Brevard Community College (now East Florida State College) and go on to Major in Molecular Biology/ Microbiology before he completed a Bachelor of Arts in History.

He has since become an English teacher and has taught in Alamogordo, New Mexico, Tianjin, China, and currently is teaching in Chongqing, China. No he did not make the name up.

Made in the USA
Columbia, SC
29 January 2021